ART DECO DESIGNS

IN COLOR

EDITED BY CHARLES RAHN FRY

DOVER PUBLICATIONS, INC., NEW YORK

INTRODUCTION

Between 1913 and 1932 in Paris, a number of spectacular portfolios of decorative compositions, featuring the work of the city's leading artist-designers, were produced by the pochoir stencil technique. The albums range in mood from E. A. Seguy's 1914 *Floréal*, a marvel of brilliant intensity influenced by the flamboyant, gaudy colors popularized by the Ballets Russes, to V. Boberman's 1929 *Tapis*, a collection of designs done entirely in "sad colors"—grays, tans, browns and blues—which depend for sophistication on contrasts of value and depth rather than hue. Other master practitioners were E. Benedictus, S. Delaunay, S. Gladky and G. Valmier, whose compositions illustrate the scope of decorative versatility of the era. Color influences also derived from the early twentieth-century art movements of the Fauves, Die Brücke, and others who championed flat colors in novel relationships.

The pochoir process was essentially a stencil method of color reproduction. While simple in concept, the technique became complex in practice. Like lithography and serigraphy, its purpose was to multiply an image. The creation of the image, of course, was the province of the artist or designer. Once this was achieved, the pochoir craftsman became involved. He cut the stencils, mixed the paint, selected the paper, determined the succession of applications and applied the medium in conjunction with the artist. Like much printmaking of today, it was a group effort. While pochoir prints were seldom signed or numbered, research suggests that albums were produced in quantities ranging from a few hundred up to as many as a thousand.

Unlike most standard methods of reproduction, pochoir permitted flexibility from print to print. Since the paint medium was applied by hand, blue could give way to green in a given area. Evenness of tone could change to gradation. Solidity could be broken by additional free-hand art work. There was potential for variation, for uniqueness, for the one-of-a-kind. The manual application of water color, gouache, oil or metallic paint, and the edge frequently made by the medium flowing into the stencil, provided for an exceptional freshness of appearance not found in other graphic reproduction methods. Pochoir prints sometimes required as many as 80 different stencils. The bright, unbroken color expanses permitted sharp, unmuddied reproduction for varied applications; the present book is an example.

Among several firms that specialized in pochoir, the Maison J. Saudé was recognized as the foremost. M. Saudé's superb 1925 treatise on the subject, *Le Traité d'Enluminure d'Art au Pochoir*, published in an edition of only 500 copies, remains the definitive explanation of the technique.

With the onset of the world depression in the 1930's, this deluxe method of color reproduction became too costly to continue on a large scale. It appears to have been replaced to some extent by the silk screen or serigraphic technique, a more mechanical and less expensive type of graphic reproduction—one that employed a press instead of the manual skills of many craftsmen.

Our reproductions are from the following portfolios, all published in Paris (the plate numbers given are those of the present volume):

Album N° 1 par Georges Valmier, Aux Editions Albert Lévy, n.d. [1930?] (Plates 36—46).

Dessins: 20 planches en couleurs, Librairie des Arts Décoratifs, n.d. [1930?] (Plates 6, 7, 26).

Fleurs de Serge Gladky, Editions "Synth," 1929, (title page, Plate 15).

Idées 1 de Jacques Camus: douze planches, Librairie des Arts Décoratifs, n.d. (Plate 8).

Inspirations: 80 motifs en couleur; A. Garcelon, Ch. Massin et Cie, Editeurs, n.d. (Plates 11—14).

Nouvelles compositions décoratives, 1re série: 48 planches par Serge Gladky, Editions d'Art Charles Moreau, n.d. (Plates 16—25).

Prismes: 40 planches de dessins et coloris nouvaux; E. A. Seguy, Editions d'Art Charles Moreau, n.d. [1931] (Plates 27—35).

Relais 1930: quinze planches donnant quarante-deux motifs décoratifs; Benedictus, Editions Vincent, Freal et Cie, n.d. [1930] (Plates 1—4).

Sonia Delaunay: ses peintures, ses objets, ses tissus simultanés, ses modes, Librairie des Arts Décoratifs, n.d. [1925] (Plates 9, 10).

Tapis: vingt-quatre compositions en couleurs; V. Boberman, Editions des Quatre Chemins, 1929 (Plate 5).

New York City   Charles Rahn Fry
1975

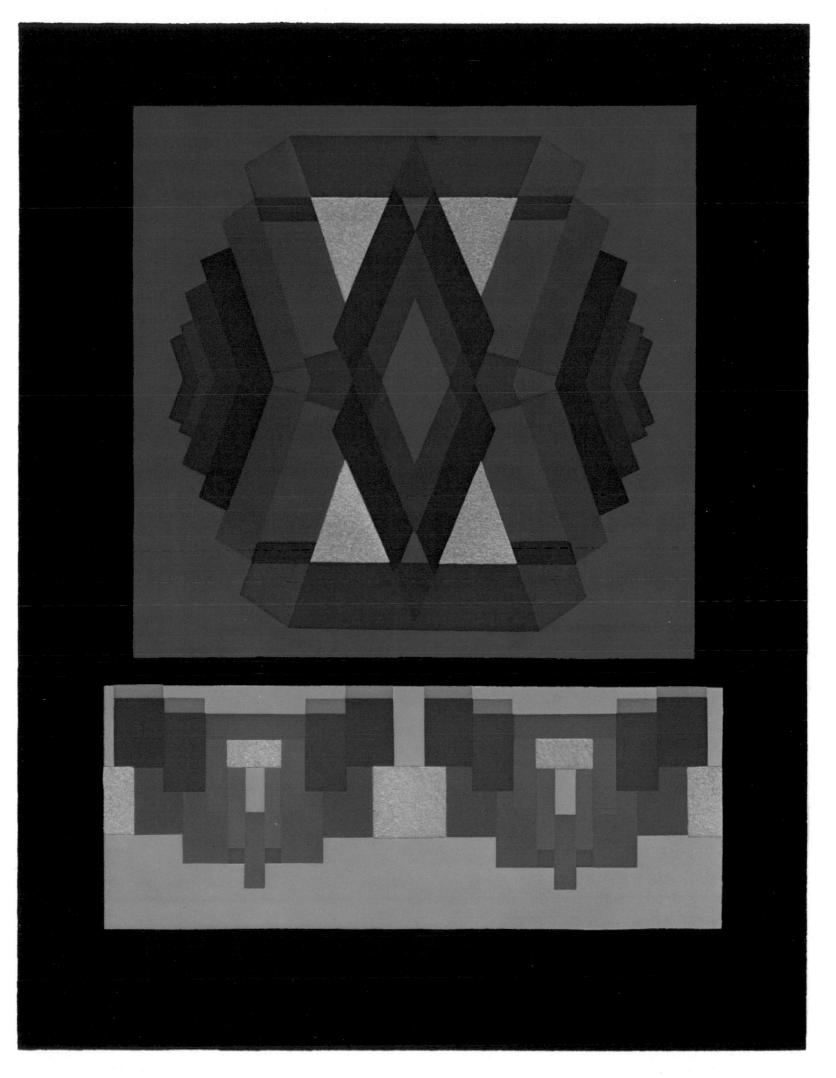

Edouard Benedictus　1

2   Edouard Benedictus

Edouard Benedictus   3

4   Edouard Benedictus

V. Boberman   5

A. Garcelon   11

A. Garcelon   13

14   A. Garcelon

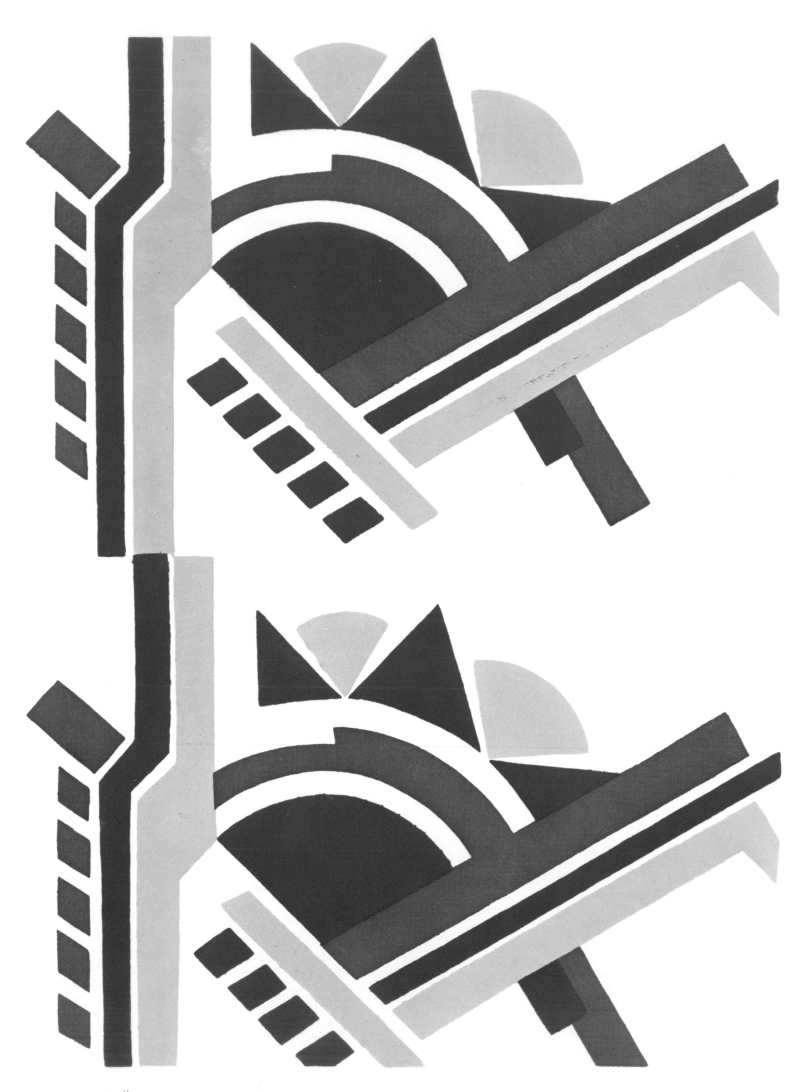

16   Serge Gladky

18   Serge Gladky

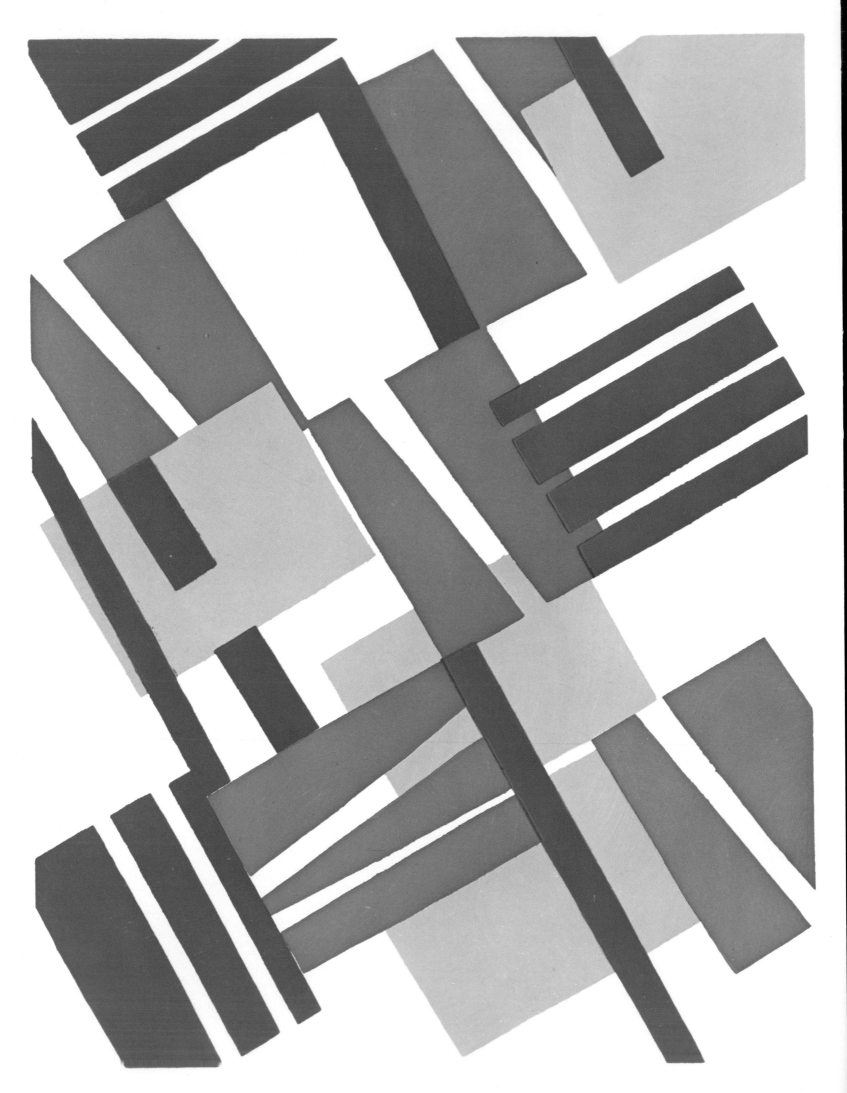

Serge Gladky

Serge Gladky   21

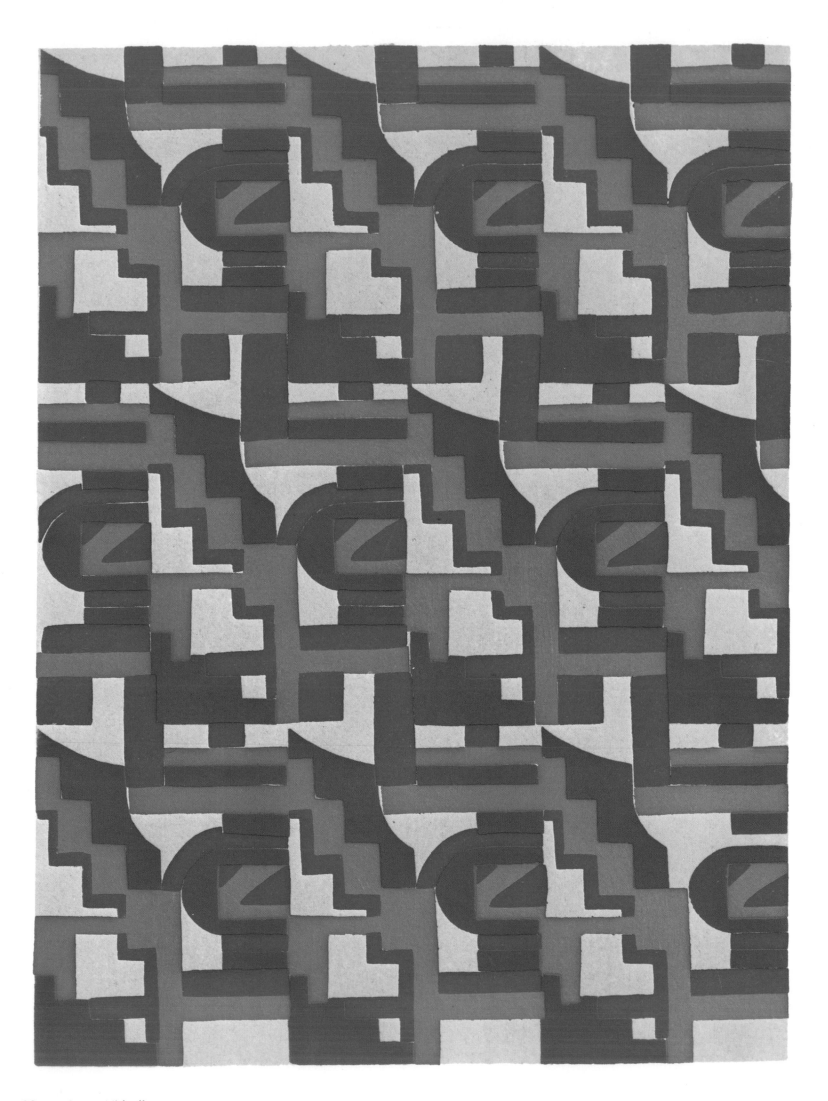

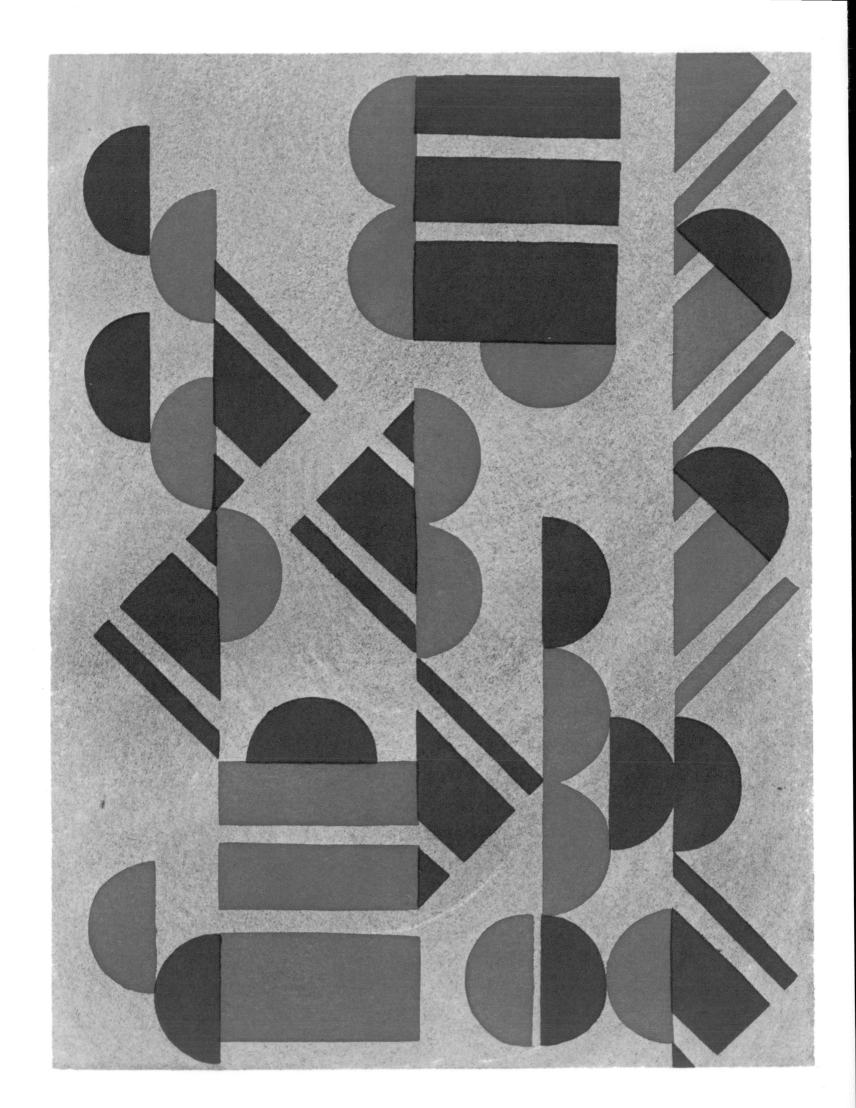

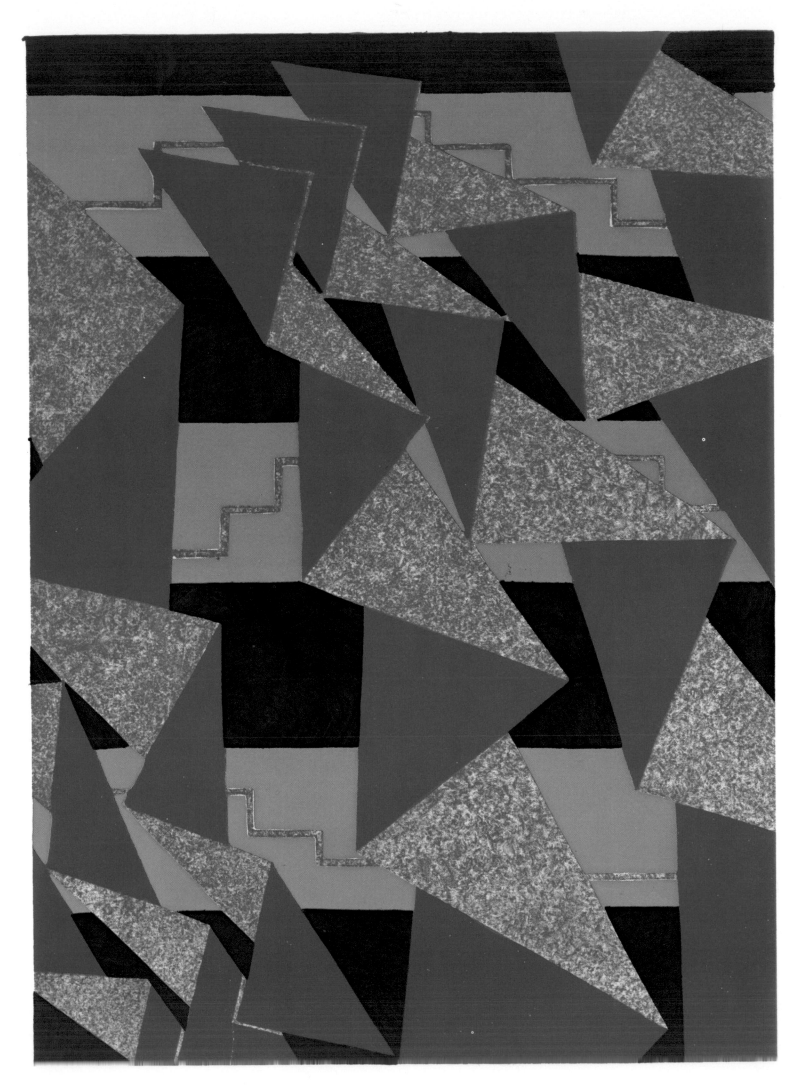

30   E. A. Seguy

32   E. A. Seguy

34   E. A. Seguy

Georges Valmier

Georges Valmier 37

Georges Valmier 39

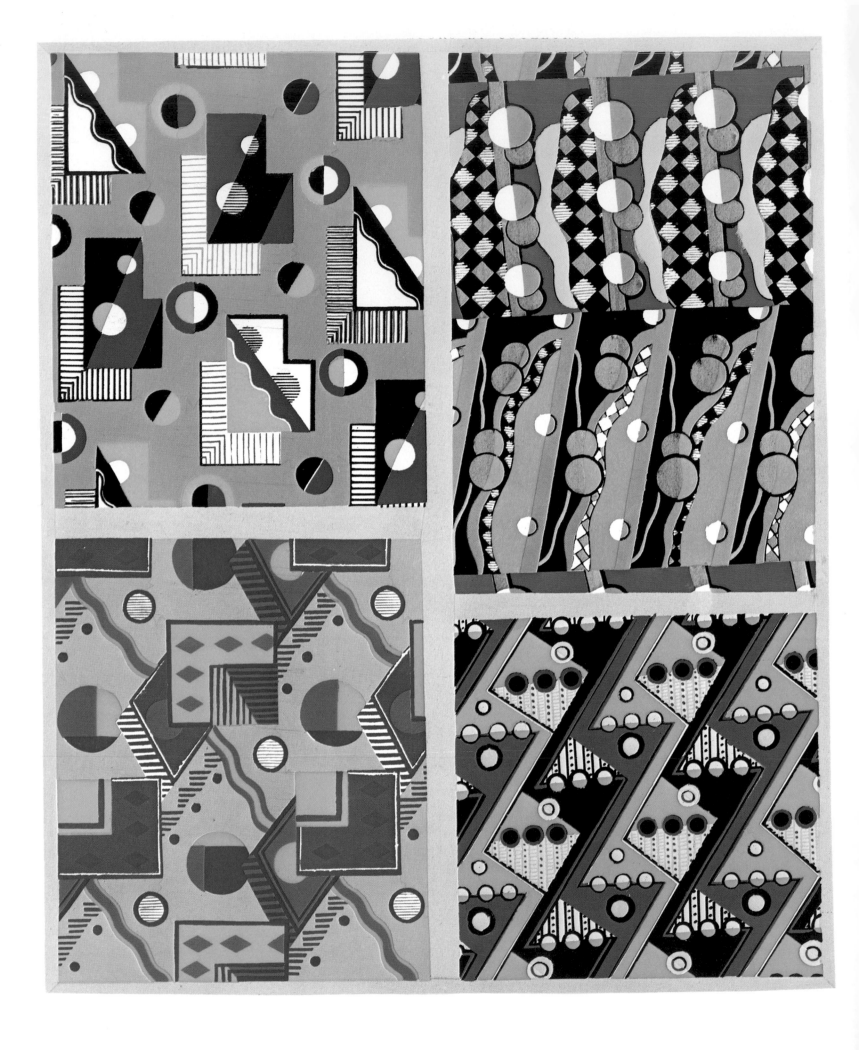

42   Georges Valmier

44   Georges Valmier

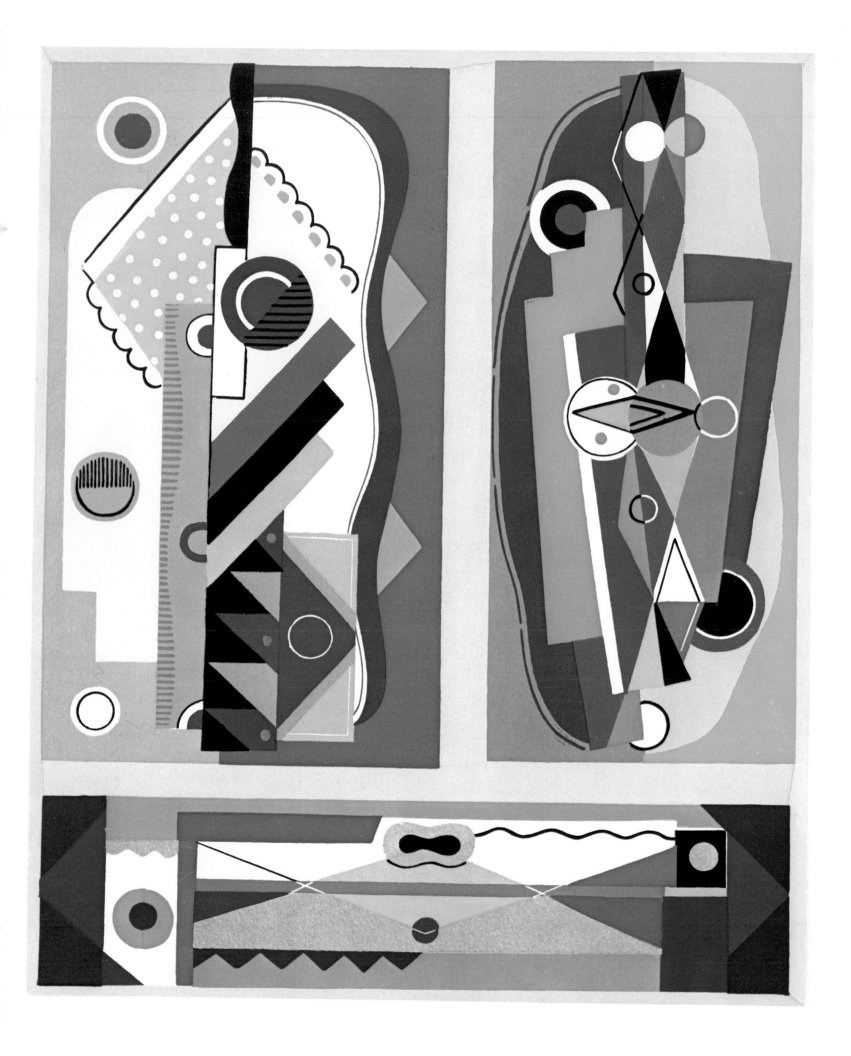

46   Georges Valmier